I0080901

This Is for the Sistan's

a Biblical Guide to

Understanding Men

By
Pastor Henry Owens Jr

**Copyright @2025 Pastor Henry Owens Jr
All Rights Reserved**

Table Of Content

Foreword

In 2008 I moved from Flint Michigan to Reno Nevada. That's right, Reno, Nevada! I moved to Reno because of a job promotion from the company I worked for. Shortly after my arrival I found a great church home in Greater Light Christian Center. It was there that I met Henry Owens. I often joke that Henry and I became friends because my first thought when meeting him was, "Something is wrong with this Brother!" This sparked our friendship since there was something wrong with me too! But I realized that what was wrong with us was actually right for the world!

As our relationship developed, our friendship grew stronger. I recall a particular incident that significantly impacted our bond. After completing a round of golf one day, while we were driving home, he spontaneously suggested, "Let us go and pick up a gift for our wives." "Pick up a gift for our wives?' I remember thinking about all the friends I've had in my life; I had never had a friend who made such a suggestion. In the midst of joking, clowning on each other and having fun this man paused to prioritize his wife. This experience that was entirely new to me.

In retrospect it is likely the small gestures of love like the one mentioned above and countless insights gained through years of successful marriage that have equipped Henry to author this book. In today's era of complex relationships and continually evolving societal norms, the importance of a husband and wife truly understanding one another remains paramount. This book takes its reader on a profound journey through Scripture, offering wisdom, guidance, and clarity on the nature of women, their roles, and how we can embrace a more meaningful understanding of them through a biblical perspective.

Throughout history women have been celebrated, misunderstood, empowered, and at times overlooked. The Bible provides foundational truths that illuminate their strength, purpose, value and significance. Whether you are seeking insight for marriage, friendship, or simply a deeper comprehension of the divine design of womanhood, this book will guide you with biblical principles rooted in love, respect, and wisdom.

I encourage you to engage with these pages with an open heart, an open mind, and a desire to learn. Do not merely read the content but compare it with your own thoughts and feelings. The ultimate objective should not be solely to acquire knowledge, but to be transformed by the insights gained. This book aims to serve as a source of reflection and revelation, enhancing your understanding of the women in your life and promoting a Christ-centered perspective in all relationships.

Pastor Lenard Dotson

Associate Pastor, Family Worship Center Church International, Flint Michigan

April 18, 2025

Dedication

I want to dedicate this book to my Lord and Savior, Jesus Christ.

Also, I would like to dedicate this book to my wife, Latrice L. Owens. Thank you for all your encouragement and support.

To my daughters Tatiyanna L. Owens and Brittany M. Owens/Ellis, and to my seven granddaughters who bring me so much joy.

Acknowledgments

I want to acknowledge my Lord and Savior, Jesus Christ. Without His wisdom, none of this would have been possible.

My wife Latrice L. Owens, my children Tatiyanna Owens and Brittany Ellis, and my seven granddaughters Amiyah Jackson, Layanna Ellis, A'sani Ellis, Serenity Ellis, Grace Ellis, Zyiah Ellis, and Zariah Matthews—I love you!

My father and mother in the Gospel, Pastor Glenn & Gwen Taylor of Reno, NV, thank you for your encouragement over the years.

Elder Waterford of Los Angeles, CA, helped me obtain my ministry license. Minister Bowers of Los Angeles, CA, encouraged me to preach the Gospel in my youth.

My three sisters, Myrdle Broughton, Samantha Butler, and Patricia Owens (who has gone home to be with the Lord).

My mother, Clester Willis-Jefferson, who has gone on to be with the Lord, inspired me to evangelize the world with my aunt and her twin sister, Vester Moore.

My brothers in life: Lenard and Monique Dotson, Matthew and Rhonda Knight, Anthony and Loretta Velasquez, Vincent Stewart, Glenn Taylor II, Eddie Butler, Mitchell and Geishula Moore Jr., Terrell and Tara Taylor, and Tabu and Ebony McKnight.

Special Thanks to my wife Latrice for this Forward

About the Author

Pastor Henry Owens Jr. grew up in church as a child prodigy and was called and licensed in ministry at the age of twelve.

He has studied the books of Daniel and Revelation for more than thirty years and has served in four churches across over forty years of ministry in various leadership roles, all by the grace of God.

He currently hosts weekly live Bible study sessions on YouTube and Facebook, where his teaching and evangelistic style reach believers worldwide.

He and his wife, Latrice L. Owens, have been married for thirty-five years and are the proud parents of two daughters and seven granddaughters. His mission is to strengthen families, empower women through understanding, and restore biblical love and unity within the body of Christ.

Synopsis

In a world where women often struggle to find their voice, worth, and value, This Is for the Sistah offers biblical truth, encouragement, and healing. Pastor Henry Owens Jr. writes with compassion, humor, and pastoral wisdom, drawing from decades of ministry to illuminate the heart of God toward His daughters.

This book helps women rediscover their God-given identity and teaches men to see women as divine creations to be honored, loved, and respected. Through Scripture and practical teaching, Pastor Owens explores:

- The strength of a woman rooted in faith.
- The power of forgiveness and emotional healing.
- The beauty of divine womanhood and self-worth.
- The importance of understanding and communication in relationships.
- How God restores broken hearts and renews inner confidence.

More than a message—it's a movement of restoration. This Is for the Sistah reminds every woman that she is loved, valued, and purposed by God. It is a call to healing, empowerment, and divine self-discovery.

This Is for The Sistah's

Opening: Why This Book Matters

Sisters, this book is for you! Whether you're 8 or 80, whether you are single, married, divorced, or seeking clarity about the men in your life, this book is designed to empower, enlighten, and equip you to understand and engage with men in a biblical, practical, and transformative way.

Have you ever wondered why men seem so different in how they express love, handle stress, or lead their families? Have you ever felt frustrated, confused, or disconnected when trying to communicate with the men in your life? If so, you are not alone. But here's the good news: God did not create men and women to live in conflict—He designed us to complement one another, to build together, and to thrive in harmony.

In today's world, we are bombarded with false narratives about what manhood and masculinity should look like. Society tries to redefine what God has already established. This book will guide you through the truth of God's Word about men—how they are wired spiritually, emotionally, mentally, physically, financially, and scientifically—and how women can engage, support, and inspire them without losing themselves in the process.

💡 *Did you know that men don't always say what they feel, but they always show it?* 💡 *Did you know that when a man is struggling financially, he often feels like he is failing in life?* 💡 *Did you know that respect is a man's love language—even more than words of affection?* 💡 *Did you know that men experience emotions just as deeply as women, but they often lack the tools to express them?*

This book is here to break the cycle of misunderstanding. It will help you see men through a new lens—God's lens. You will gain insight into how men think, how they process emotions, how they love, what they need, and how women can bring out the best in them.

This is not just a book about relationships—it is a book about understanding the divine order of manhood and womanhood. It will challenge you, inspire you, and equip you with wisdom that will shape how you engage with men for the rest of your life.

Get ready to learn, grow, and transform through God's wisdom about men—so you can build stronger relationships, healthier families, and a deeper spiritual understanding of the world God designed for both men and women.

Are you ready? Let's dive in!

Chapter 1:
God's Blueprint for Men

God's Divine Design

From the very beginning, God created men with a unique and essential purpose. He designed them to be leaders, protectors, and providers—not out of dominance, but out of responsibility. A man's role in the family, community, and world is significant, yet over time, culture and society have distorted and challenged his identity.

Many men today struggle with understanding their purpose, and as a result, they drift through life without clear direction. When a man does not fully understand his God-given role, he may feel lost, restless, or inadequate. A woman who understands a man's divine blueprint can support, encourage, and uplift him rather than unknowingly contributing to his struggles.

If you have ever wondered:

💡 Why do men struggle with expressing emotions?

💡 Why do men prioritize work and purpose so deeply?

💡 Why does respect mean more to men than affection?

💡 Why do some men seem to withdraw rather than communicate?

Then this chapter will provide answers rooted in biblical truth.

Biblical Foundation

God created men and women in His image, yet He gave each gender distinct roles that complement one another. Understanding the biblical foundation of manhood is the key to understanding why men function the way they do.

1. Men Were Created in God's Image

📖 Genesis 1:27 – "So God created mankind in His own image, in the image of God He created them; male and female He created them."

This verse establishes that men and women are equal in value, but they are not identical in function. Just as God has both justice and mercy, strength and gentleness, He designed men and women to reflect different aspects of His nature.

• Men reflect God's strength, leadership, and provision.
• Women reflect God's nurturing, wisdom, and relational nature.

This is why when a man walks in his divine calling, he embodies God's strength and leadership, and when a woman understands his design, she can uplift and encourage him rather than resist him.

2. Men Are Called to Lead with Responsibility

📖 1 Corinthians 11:3 – "But I want you to realize that the head of every man is Christ, and the head of the woman is man, and the head of Christ is God."

This verse is often misunderstood—it does not imply male superiority, but rather divine order. Just as Christ leads with humility and love, men are called to lead with wisdom, patience, and service.

- Leadership is not about control—it is about guidance and responsibility.
- A godly man does not demand submission—he inspires it through his character.
- A woman who understands this will see leadership as a blessing, not a burden.

When a man walks in his God-ordained leadership, he creates security, stability, and peace in his home and relationships.

3. Men Were Given the Role of Work and Protection

📖 Genesis 2:15 – "The Lord God took the man and put him in the Garden of Eden to work it and take care of it."

Before Eve was even created, Adam was given a responsibility—to work and care for God's creation. This shows that men are naturally wired to build, sustain, and protect.

- A man's work is tied to his identity—when he cannot provide, he often struggles emotionally.
- A man needs to feel useful and productive—if he lacks purpose, he becomes restless.
- A woman who supports his work and vision helps him thrive.

A woman who understands this won't view a man's work as neglect—instead, she will recognize that his drive to build is part of his divine calling.

Key Truths About Men

Understanding a man's design, struggles, and needs will strengthen relationships and eliminate unnecessary conflict. Here are three fundamental truths about men:

1. Men Are Created to Lead with Love and Wisdom

Leadership is in a man's spiritual DNA—he is meant to be a protector, a guide, and a source of strength. However, leadership is not about dominance; it is about responsibility and servanthood.

📖 Ephesians 5:25 – "Husbands, love your wives, just as Christ loved the church and gave himself up for her."

A godly man:

✅ Leads his home with love and humility.

✅ Protects his wife and children physically, emotionally, and spiritually.

✅ Provides not just financially, but also emotionally and spiritually.

A woman's support and respect help a man become the leader God designed him to be.

2. Men Are Driven by Purpose and Need a Vision to Thrive

📖 Proverbs 29:18 – "Where there is no vision, the people perish."

Men are goal-oriented—they need to work towards something greater. A man without a mission or direction often feels lost and disconnected.

When a woman encourages a man's dreams, she is fueling his purpose. If she dismisses or belittles his ambitions, he may shut down or withdraw emotionally.

3. Men Struggle When They Lack Affirmation and Direction

Men rarely verbalize their need for encouragement, but it is vital to their well-being.

- Encouragement from a woman fuels his confidence.
- Words of respect and admiration uplift him.
- Criticism and nagging drain him emotionally.

  📖 Proverbs 27:17 – "Iron sharpens iron, and one man sharpens another."

  A man thrives in an environment where he is affirmed and respected.

What Women Need to Know

Many women misinterpret a man's actions because they do not fully understand his internal struggles.

1. A Man Without Purpose Is Often Restless and Frustrated

- If a man seems distant or unmotivated, it may be because he feels directionless.
- Instead of criticizing him, a woman can help him seek God's purpose.
- Encouraging his spiritual and personal growth strengthens the relationship.

2. Men Seek Respect Over Affection—Affirmation Fuels Their Drive

📖 *Ephesians 5:33* – "The wife must respect her husband."

- Women often desire love and emotional connection, while men crave respect and affirmation.
- Respect does not mean submission without boundaries—it means valuing his leadership, hard work, and character.
- Simple words like "I appreciate you" or "Thank you for working so hard for us" can mean more to a man than "I love you."

3. Men Will Often Suffer in Silence Rather Than Admit Weakness

- Society teaches men to be strong and self-sufficient, so they often hide their struggles.
- Many women assume silence means indifference, but it often means he is processing deeply.
- A woman who creates a safe space for him to open up allows him to trust and be vulnerable.

Final Thoughts

A man who understands and accepts his God-given identity is empowered to lead, love, and protect in a way that honors God and blesses those around him. When a woman recognizes and supports a man's divine purpose, she partners with God's plan for him, creating an environment where he can thrive spiritually, emotionally, and mentally.

Chapter 2:
The Spiritual Mandate for Men

God's Calling for Men to Lead Spiritually

Men are not just called to be physical providers or protectors; they are commanded to be spiritual leaders in their homes, churches, and communities. When a man walks in his spiritual authority, he brings strength, stability, and guidance to his family and those around him. However, when he neglects this role, confusion and disorder can follow.

Today, many men struggle with their spiritual identity. Some have grown up without examples of godly men leading in faith. Others feel unequipped or inadequate to take on the responsibility of being the spiritual head. Yet, God has provided clear instructions on what He expects from men, and He gives them the grace to fulfill this high calling.

A woman who understands the spiritual struggles men face can become a powerful source of support, encouragement, and prayer for the men in her life.

Biblical Foundation

1. Men Must Stand Firm in Faith

📖 1 Corinthians 16:13 – "Be on your guard; stand firm in the faith; be courageous; be strong."

A spiritually strong man does not waver in his faith, even in the face of challenges. God calls men to:

- Be vigilant against spiritual attacks.
- Stand firm in what they believe, despite opposition.
- Show courage in their faith, leading with confidence.

Many men today struggle with doubt and fear of failure. Society tells them to depend on their own strength, but the Bible teaches that true strength comes from depending on God.

2. A Man's Leadership Starts in His Home

📖 Joshua 24:15 – "As for me and my house, we will serve the Lord."

Men are not just called to lead themselves; they are called to lead their families. Joshua made a bold declaration that his household would serve the Lord, setting an example for all men.

When a man prioritizes faith in his home:

- His wife feels secure, knowing she has a partner in faith.
- His children grow up with spiritual stability.
- His home becomes a place of peace and protection.

3. The Husband as the Spiritual Head

📖 Ephesians 5:23 – "For the husband is the head of the wife as Christ is the head of the church, his body, of which he is the Savior."

This verse has been misunderstood by many, but biblical headship is not about control—it is about responsibility. Just as Christ leads the Church with sacrificial love, a husband must lead his home with humility, grace, and strength.

A spiritually strong husband:

- Prays over his wife and children.
- Seeks wisdom from God before making decisions.
- Leads by example, not by force.

A wife who honors her husband's leadership helps him grow in confidence and walk in his spiritual calling.

What Women Need to Know

Many women become **frustrated** when they feel their husband, father, or son **is not leading spiritually**. However, understanding **why men struggle** in this area can lead to more **effective support and encouragement**.

1. A Spiritually Weak Man May Struggle with Decision-Making and Confidence

When a man is disconnected from God, he:

- Feels uncertain about his decisions.
- Lacks the wisdom needed to lead his family.
- Is more prone to discouragement and stress.

Rather than criticizing his lack of spiritual leadership, a woman can encourage him by: ✓ Speaking words of life and encouragement. ✓ Asking for his input on spiritual matters. ✓ Gently reminding him of God's calling on his life.

2. A Woman's Prayer and Encouragement Can Help Guide a Man's Faith

📖 James 5:16 – "The prayer of a righteous person is powerful and effective."

Many men will never admit they are struggling spiritually. But a woman's prayers and encouragement can have a lasting impact.

Ways to support a man spiritually:

- Pray for him daily—even when he doesn't ask for it.
- Encourage him to seek God's wisdom in decisions.
- Speak faith over his life instead of discouragement.

3. Men Need to See Faith in Action, Not Just Hear About It

📖 1 Peter 3:1 – "Wives, in the same way, submit yourselves to your own husbands so that, if any of them do not believe the word, they may be won over without words by the behavior of their wives."

If a man is struggling spiritually, arguing or forcing him into faith won't work. Instead, a woman should live out her faith in a way that inspires him.

What this looks like: ✅ Modeling peace and trust in God—showing him what faith looks like. ✅ Being patient—understanding that spiritual growth takes time. ✅ Allowing God to work on his heart—instead of trying to "fix" him.

Real-Life Applications

Biblical Example: Abraham and Sarah

📖 Genesis 18:19 – "For I have chosen him, that he may command his children and his household after him to keep the way of the Lord by doing righteousness and justice."

Abraham is known as a great man of faith, but his journey was not perfect. There were times when he doubted and made mistakes. However, God still used him as the father of nations.

Sarah, his wife, supported him by:

- Trusting in God's promises.
- Encouraging him when he felt discouraged.
- Following his leadership, even when it required faith.

A man does not have to be perfect to be a great spiritual leader—he just needs to keep seeking God.

Modern-Day Example: A Wife Encouraging Her Husband's Spiritual Growth

Imagine a husband who does not prioritize prayer or church. His wife feels frustrated and alone in her spiritual walk. Instead of nagging him or pushing him, she:

1. **Prays for him daily**, asking God to stir his heart.
2. **Invites him to small spiritual activities**, like reading a verse together or attending church without pressure.
3. **Shows patience and love**, trusting that God will move in His timing.

Over time, her quiet faith influences him, and he begins to take steps toward God.

Practical Ways to Support a Man's Spiritual Growth

For Wives:

✅ Pray for him daily, even if he doesn't ask. ✅ Encourage him to make spiritual decisions in the home. ✅ Respect his efforts, even if he is not perfect.

For Mothers Raising Sons:

✅ Teach them the Word of God from an early age. ✅ Encourage them to pray and seek wisdom. ✅ Model faith so they see it in action.

For Sisters, Friends, or Mentors:

✅ Uplift the men around you with encouragement. ✅ Remind them of their God-given purpose. ✅ Be patient with their spiritual growth.

Final Thoughts

God calls men to be spiritual leaders, but many feel unequipped or uncertain about their role. A woman's prayer, encouragement, and example can help strengthen a man's faith and give him the confidence to walk in his divine calling.

💡 Sisters, your influence is powerful! As you pray for and support the men in your life, you help them grow into the spiritual leaders God has called them to be.

Chapter 3:
The Emotional World of Men

Understanding the Depth of a Man's Emotions

Many believe that men are emotionally distant or incapable of deep feelings. However, the truth is that men feel just as deeply as women, but they express emotions differently. Society often discourages men from openly expressing emotions, leading them to internalize their struggles rather than seek support. As a result, men are sometimes seen as cold, detached, or unfeeling, when in reality, they are processing their emotions in a different way.

A woman who understands how men process emotions can create an environment where a man feels safe to express himself, rather than pressured or judged. When a man knows he is truly heard and understood, it strengthens his relationships, his confidence, and his ability to lead effectively.

Biblical Foundation

📖 Proverbs 27:19 – "As in water face reflects face, so the heart of man reflects man."

A man's heart reflects his inner struggles, joys, and concerns. However, because many men are taught to hide vulnerability, they do not always share what is in their hearts. This does not mean they do not feel—rather, they are often processing in silence.

📖 Ephesians 5:25 – "Husbands, love your wives, just as Christ loved the church and gave Himself up for her."

Men show love through actions and sacrifice rather than words. A man may not always say, "I love you", but his actions—working tirelessly, fixing things, protecting his family—are his expressions of love.

Understanding how God designed men to process and express emotions will help women better communicate, support, and encourage the men in their lives.

How Men Process Emotion

Unlike women, who often process emotions externally by talking things through, men process internally. Many men struggle to articulate their emotions, not because they don't feel, but because they have not been taught how to express their emotions in words.

1. Men Often Suppress Emotions to Avoid Appearing Weak

- From childhood, many boys are told to "man up" or "stop crying."
- Expressing vulnerability is often viewed as a sign of weakness.
- Men may bury feelings instead of processing them, which can lead to frustration, stress, and even depression.

2. Many Men Don't Have the Vocabulary to Articulate Their Feelings

- Women are generally more comfortable discussing emotions, while men are often more comfortable acting on them.
- A man who is stressed, fearful, or anxious may not say, "I'm overwhelmed." Instead, he may become withdrawn, irritable, or distracted.

- It is important for women to recognize non-verbal signs of distress rather than expecting a man to always put his feelings into words.

3. Stress and Emotional Burdens Manifest in Silence or Withdrawal

- When a man is struggling, he may withdraw into silence rather than seek help.
- Instead of talking, he may immerse himself in work, sports, or hobbies as a way to cope.
- This does not mean he is rejecting his loved ones—he is processing internally.

Men need space, patience, and understanding when they are dealing with emotional burdens. Pushing them to talk before they are ready can often lead to frustration rather than healing.

What Women Need to Know

A woman who wants to support a man emotionally must understand how he operates. Instead of expecting him to process emotions like a woman, she can learn to recognize his emotional needs and create a safe space for him.

1. Patience Is Key—Pressuring a Man to Talk May Push Him Further Away

- If a man is not ready to talk, trying to force a conversation can make him feel cornered or overwhelmed.
- Instead of saying, "Why don't you ever talk to me?", try: ✓ "I'm here when you're ready." ✓ "I know you have a lot on your mind. Whenever you want to talk, I'm listening."

- Giving him time to process allows him to come forward when he feels safe to share.

2. Encouraging Safe Emotional Expression Builds Trust

📖 Proverbs 31:26 – "She speaks with wisdom, and faithful instruction is on her tongue."

- If a man feels judged or criticized when he shares his feelings, he will stop opening up.
- Encourage him by validating his emotions: ✅ "I understand why you feel that way." ✅ "I appreciate you sharing that with me." ✅ "I respect how you're handling this."
- When a man knows he is not being judged, he is more likely to open up emotionally.

3. A Man Who Shuts Down Is Not Rejecting You—He's Processing Internally

- If a man withdraws, it is not necessarily a sign that he is angry or uninterested.
- Some men need time alone to think and process.
- Instead of taking it personally, give him space while reassuring him that you are there when he's ready.

📖 Ecclesiastes 3:7 – "A time to tear and a time to mend, a time to be silent and a time to speak."

A wise woman knows when to speak and when to give space, trusting that the right moment for communication will come.

Practical Ways to Support a Man Emotionally

1. Learn His Love Language

📖 1 John 3:18 – "Let us not love with words or speech but with actions and in truth."

- Men often show love through actions more than words.
- Recognizing how he expresses love will help you understand how he wants to receive love.
- If he values acts of service, doing small things for him shows care.
- If he values physical touch, a hug or gentle touch may mean more than words.

2. Be a Source of Peace, Not Pressure

📖 Proverbs 21:19 – "Better to live in a desert than with a quarrelsome and nagging wife."

- A man often deals with many pressures—work, financial responsibilities, societal expectations.
- He needs home to be a place of peace, not another source of stress.
- Encouraging words and patience create a peaceful atmosphere where he feels safe.

3. Pray for Him, Even When He Doesn't Ask

📖 James 5:16 – "The prayer of a righteous person is powerful and effective."

- Many men struggle in silence, carrying burdens they don't express.

- Praying over your husband, father, or son invites God's strength into their emotional battles.
- Even if he doesn't verbalize it, knowing he is being covered in prayer strengthens him.

Final Thoughts

Men are not emotionally detached—they simply process and express emotions differently than women. Understanding this fosters stronger relationships and deeper trust.

💡 Sisters, you have more influence than you realize! By creating a safe, judgment-free space, speaking words of encouragement, and allowing men to process in their own way, you help them become more emotionally secure, confident, and open.

As you navigate relationships with the men in your life, remember: Love with patience, listen with wisdom, and trust God to work in their hearts.

Chapter 4: Understanding a Woman's Sexuality and Intimacy Needs

God's Design for Intimacy

Intimacy in marriage is more than a physical connection—it is a sacred union designed by God. True intimacy is built on love, respect, emotional connection, and spiritual unity. When intimacy is reduced to a mere physical act, it loses its depth and purpose. For a woman, intimacy is not just about desire; it is about feeling cherished, secure, and emotionally connected to her husband.

📖 1 Corinthians 7:3-5 – "The husband should fulfill his marital duty to his wife, and likewise the wife to her husband. The wife does not have authority over her own body but yields it to her husband. In the same way, the husband does not have authority over his own body but yields it to his wife. Do not deprive each other except by mutual consent and for a time, so that you may devote yourselves to prayer. Then come together again so that Satan will not tempt you because of your lack of self-control."

This passage teaches that intimacy is a mutual act of love and service—not something demanded or withheld as a form of control. God's design for intimacy is about oneness, sacrifice, and mutual fulfillment. A man must understand that intimacy begins long before the bedroom—it starts with emotional connection, trust, and security.

19

Biblical Example: The Song of Solomon

The **Song of Solomon** is a beautiful and passionate depiction of **love between a husband and wife**. This book of the Bible shows that God created intimacy to be sacred, joyful, and deeply fulfilling.

📖 Song of Solomon 7:10 – "I am my beloved's, and his desire is for me."

This verse illustrates the depth of intimacy where love, respect, and passion coexist in a holy bond. The relationship described in Song of Solomon demonstrates that intimacy is not just about physical desire but also about emotional and spiritual connection.

Many men struggle to understand that a woman needs to feel emotionally connected before she desires physical closeness. If a husband wants his wife to be open to intimacy, he must first engage her heart, affirm her, and create a safe emotional space where she feels valued.

Fictional Example

A husband, eager for closeness, did not realize his wife needed emotional security first. He was affectionate but did not take the time to nurture her heart, listen to her thoughts, and affirm her. Over time, she withdrew emotionally, making physical intimacy feel forced rather than natural.

One day, he decided to intentionally affirm her daily—not just in words, but in small acts of kindness. He started engaging in meaningful conversations, expressing appreciation, and helping relieve her burdens. Soon, their intimacy deepened, revealing that connection starts outside the bedroom.

This story highlights a crucial lesson: a woman's heart must be pursued before her body.

Lessons on Intimacy in Marriage

1. Emotional Connection Precedes Physical Connection

📖 Ephesians 5:25 – "Husbands, love your wives, just as Christ loved the church and gave himself up for her."

- A woman needs to feel emotionally safe before she desires physical intimacy.
- A man must nurture his wife's heart through kindness, attentiveness, and security.
- When a woman feels heard, valued, and appreciated, intimacy becomes natural rather than forced.

2. Honor and Respect Enhance Desire

📖 1 Peter 3:7 – "Husbands, in the same way be considerate as you live with your wives, and treat them with respect as the weaker partner and as heirs with you of the gracious gift of life, so that nothing will hinder your prayers."

- When a woman is disrespected, ignored, or criticized, she will naturally withdraw.
- If a man desires a strong intimate connection, he must honor his wife's thoughts, feelings, and boundaries.
- Respect cultivates trust, which leads to genuine, joyful intimacy.

3. True Intimacy Reflects God's Love for His People

📖 Genesis 2:24 – "That is why a man leaves his father and mother and is united to his wife, and they become one flesh."

- Marriage is a reflection of God's covenant with His people.
- True intimacy is not just physical—it is spiritual, emotional, and relational.
- A man must lead in love, just as Christ loves the Church, for his marriage to flourish.

What Men Need to Understand About a Woman's Needs

Men often focus on physical aspects of intimacy, while women seek emotional security first. Here are three truths men must understand:

1. A Woman's Desire is Deeply Connected to Emotional Security

- If a woman feels unheard or emotionally neglected, she will struggle with intimacy.
- Small gestures—a listening ear, an encouraging word, or helping with responsibilities—build trust and connection.
- A woman desires to be cherished, not just desired physically.

2. Intimacy is About Giving, Not Just Receiving

📖 Acts 20:35 – "It is more blessed to give than to receive."

- Intimacy is not one-sided—it is about serving and loving one another.
- When a man prioritizes his wife's heart, she will naturally respond with openness.
- Love should be expressed daily—not just when physical intimacy is desired.

3. Women Need Consistency, Not Just Moments of Passion

- Women thrive in emotional consistency.
- Intimacy should not be transactional but an ongoing expression of love and unity.
- A woman needs to know that her husband's love does not fade outside the bedroom.

Practical Ways to Strengthen Intimacy

For Husbands:

✅ Pursue her emotionally—ask about her day, listen to her heart. ✅ Help ease her burdens—small acts of service speak volumes. ✅ Speak words of affirmation—remind her that she is valued and loved. ✅ Pray with her—spiritual intimacy strengthens emotional and physical intimacy.

For Wives:

✅ Express appreciation for his love and efforts. ✅ Encourage intimacy rather than seeing it as an obligation. ✅ Communicate your emotional needs clearly and kindly. ✅ Pray for a deeper connection in your marriage.

Final Thoughts

Understanding a woman's emotional and intimacy needs is essential for a thriving marriage. God designed intimacy to be a reflection of His love, full of joy, mutual respect, and deep connection.

💡 Sisters, intimacy is more than a physical act—it is a sacred bond that mirrors God's love. When pursued with respect, love, and care, it becomes a beautiful expression of unity and devotion.

As you grow in your understanding of God's design for intimacy, may your marriage be filled with joy, passion, and deep spiritual connection.

Chapter 5:
The Power of a Woman's Influence

Women Shape Homes and Societies

Women have a profound impact on the spiritual, emotional, and moral direction of their families and communities. A woman's words, actions, and faith can build up or tear down the people around her. Whether as a wife, mother, sister, or friend, a woman has the power to encourage, nurture, and shape the hearts of those she loves.

📖 Proverbs 14:1 – "A wise woman builds her house, but the foolish pulls it down with her hands."

This verse is a reminder that a woman's attitude, words, and choices influence the atmosphere of her home. A wise woman invests in her family with love, patience, and encouragement, while a careless or bitter woman can create division and destruction.

Many women underestimate the influence they have over the men in their lives. A woman who understands her God-given role can uplift, inspire, and bring out the best in the men around her, leading to stronger marriages, families, and communities.

Biblical Example: Queen Esther

Queen Esther is a powerful example of a woman who used her influence for good. Though she was placed in a difficult and uncertain position, she used her wisdom, patience, and courage to change history.

📖 Esther 4:14 – "And who knows but that you have come to your royal position for such a time as this?"

Esther's story teaches us that: ✅ A woman's influence is strongest when guided by wisdom. ✅ Patience and discernment are more powerful than rash words. ✅ A woman who seeks God's guidance can affect generations.

Rather than acting impulsively, Esther prayed and sought wisdom before approaching the king. Her graceful and strategic actions saved the Jewish people from destruction.

A modern woman can apply this by choosing her words carefully, seeking God's wisdom, and using her influence to bring about positive change.

Fictional Example

A young wife named Rachel noticed that her husband, Daniel, struggled with self-doubt. He was a good man, but he lacked confidence in his ability to lead his family spiritually and financially. Instead of criticizing him for not stepping up, Rachel chose to speak life into him.

Every day, she offered words of encouragement:

- *"I see how hard you work for our family, and I appreciate you."*
- *"You are a great leader, and I believe in you."*
- *"I trust the decisions you make for us."*

Over time, Daniel gained confidence. He stepped into his leadership role with strength and purpose, simply because his wife chose to support and uplift him rather than tear him down.

This example teaches that a woman's words have the power to shape a man's confidence and ability to lead.

Key Takeaways on Influence

1. A Woman's Words Shape Destiny

📖 Proverbs 18:21 – "The tongue has the power of life and death, and those who love it will eat its fruit."

- A woman's words can build up or destroy her home.
- Speaking life, encouragement, and faith over the men in her life empowers them.
- Negative, critical words can diminish confidence and create distance.

A wise woman chooses her words carefully and uses them to inspire, support, and uplift.

2. Encouragement Empowers a Man's Leadership

📖 Ephesians 5:33 – "However, each one of you also must love his wife as he loves himself, and the wife must respect her husband."

- Men thrive on respect and affirmation.
- A woman's support can strengthen a man's ability to lead.
- Encouraging a man does not mean blind submission, but rather recognizing his strengths and uplifting him in his purpose.

A woman who believes in her husband's vision helps him to become the leader God designed him to be.

3. God Honors Women Who Use Their Influence for Good

📖 Proverbs 31:26 – "She speaks with wisdom, and faithful instruction is on her tongue."

- A godly woman uses wisdom in her influence.
- She seeks God's guidance before speaking or acting.
- She nurtures and strengthens her home through patience, love, and faith.

God honors women who build up rather than tear down. The way a woman handles her influence can either create harmony or division in her relationships.

Practical Ways to Use Influence Wisely

For Wives:

✅ Speak words of affirmation over your husband. ✅ Support his dreams and encourage him to seek God. ✅ Create a home filled with peace rather than criticism.

For Mothers:

✅ Teach your children about faith, character, and integrity. ✅ Model patience, wisdom, and strength in everyday situations. ✅ Pray for your children daily, covering them with God's protection and wisdom.

For Single Women:

✅ Use your influence to encourage friends and family. ✅ Lead by example, showing Christ's love in your actions. ✅ Mentor younger women, guiding them toward wisdom and faith.

Final Thoughts

A woman's influence is one of the most powerful forces in her home and community. Whether as a wife, mother, sister, or friend, her words, actions, and faith shape the people around her.

♥ Sisters, never underestimate the power of your influence! When you speak life, encourage others, and walk in wisdom, you fulfill God's divine calling for your life.

As you embrace God's design for influence, may your relationships be filled with peace, strength, and purpose.

Chapter 6:
Handling Conflict in Marriage

Conflict Is Inevitable, but Resolution Is a Choice

Every relationship experiences conflict. Disagreements will come, but how a couple handles them determines the strength of their bond. A godly marriage is not one without conflict, but one where both husband and wife are committed to resolving differences with love, patience, and wisdom.

📖 Ephesians 4:26 – "Do not let the sun go down on your wrath."

This verse reminds us of an essential truth: anger must be handled swiftly and wisely. When couples allow conflict to linger, resentment grows, and division takes root. On the other hand, when issues are addressed with a heart of humility and reconciliation, love is strengthened.

A godly woman understands that how she responds to conflict is just as important as the issue itself. Conflict should not be an opportunity to win an argument but to strengthen understanding and unity in marriage.

Biblical Example: Abigail and Nabal

One of the best biblical examples of handling conflict with wisdom is Abigail and Nabal.

📖 1 Samuel 25 tells the story of Nabal, a foolish and harsh man, and his wife Abigail, a woman of wisdom and discernment. When Nabal disrespected David and provoked his anger, Abigail quickly intervened with humility and wisdom, preventing bloodshed and disaster.

Lessons from Abigail:

✅ She did not react emotionally to her husband's foolishness.

✅ She acted quickly to resolve the conflict before it escalated.

✅ She used wisdom, humility, and grace to defuse the situation.

A woman's ability to handle conflict with wisdom and grace can prevent unnecessary pain in marriage and help guide her husband toward godly resolution.

Fictional Example

A husband and wife faced a heated disagreement about finances. Frustrated, they were tempted to raise their voices and argue. However, instead of fighting against each other, they chose to pause and pray together.

After a few moments of prayer, their anger dissolved into understanding. They talked through their concerns calmly and found a solution that honored God and strengthened their unity.

💡 The lesson? Unity comes through seeking God first. When couples prioritize peace over pride, conflict becomes an opportunity for growth.

How to Handle Conflict Wisely

1. Pause and Pray Before Speaking

📖 James 1:19 – "Everyone should be quick to listen, slow to speak, and slow to become angry."

- Before responding in anger, pause and pray.
- Ask God for wisdom and patience.
- Approach the conversation with a heart of understanding, not defense.

2. Seek Understanding Over Winning

📖 Proverbs 15:1 – "A gentle answer turns away wrath, but a harsh word stirs up anger."

- Conflict should not be about winning—it should be about resolving.
- Avoid using harsh or critical words that escalate tension.
- Listen without interrupting and try to understand your spouse's perspective.

3. Resolve Issues Quickly to Maintain Peace

📖 Colossians 3:13 – "Bear with each other and forgive one another if any of you has a grievance against someone. Forgive as the Lord forgave you."

- Do not let small issues turn into major problems.
- Be quick to forgive and let go of grudges.
- If a discussion gets too heated, take a break and revisit the issue later.

Practical Ways to Navigate Conflict in Marriage

For Wives:

✅ Speak with kindness and patience, even when frustrated.

✅ Avoid nagging or bringing up past mistakes.

✓ Focus on solutions, not blame.

For Husbands:

✓ Listen to understand, not just to respond.

✓ Take responsibility for your role in the conflict.

✓ Lead with humility and a willingness to reconcile.

Final Thoughts

A strong marriage is not one without conflict, but one where both partners are committed to resolving differences with love and wisdom. When handled correctly, conflict can strengthen communication, deepen trust, and bring a couple closer to God.

💡 Sisters, let your words bring peace and wisdom. Conflict is an opportunity to grow, not a battle to win.

As you navigate conflict in your marriage, may your heart be filled with patience, grace, and the wisdom of God.

Chapter 7: Understanding a Woman's Seasons in Life

Women Experience Emotional and Physical Seasons

Life is a journey of seasons, each bringing its own challenges, lessons, and blessings. Women, in particular, experience emotional, physical, and spiritual shifts throughout their lives, and these transitions require understanding, patience, and adaptability from both themselves and the people around them.

📖 Ecclesiastes 3:1 – "To everything, there is a season, a time for every purpose under heaven."

Women go through different life stages, and each season carries unique needs, struggles, and joys. Understanding these transitions allows husbands, fathers, and family members to provide the right kind of support, encouragement, and love.

Biblical Example: Naomi and Ruth

Naomi experienced profound loss and sorrow when her husband and sons died, leaving her widowed and without provision. Yet, through the unwavering support of Ruth, she found renewal and restoration.

📖 Ruth 1:16 – "But Ruth replied, 'Don't urge me to leave you or to turn back from you. Where you go I will go, and where you stay I will stay. Your people will be my people and your God my God.'"

Lessons from Naomi and Ruth:

✔ Women need strong support systems in seasons of loss and change.

✔ Companionship and loyalty bring healing during difficult transitions.

✔ God restores what is lost, often through the relationships He places in our lives.

Women thrive when they are surrounded by encouraging and faithful loved ones, just as Ruth was a source of hope and security for Naomi.

The Different Seasons of a Woman's Life

Women experience significant emotional, physical, and spiritual changes throughout their lives. Below are key seasons that impact a woman's journey.

1. Youth and Early Adulthood: Seeking Identity and Purpose

📖 Jeremiah 29:11 – "For I know the plans I have for you, declares the Lord, plans to prosper you and not to harm you, plans to give you hope and a future."

- Young women seek identity, validation, and purpose.
- They often face insecurities about self-worth, relationships, and career paths.
- Support from family, mentors, and community helps guide them into a secure and confident adulthood.

◆ **What They Need:** Encouragement, mentorship, and affirmation of their God-given potential.

2. Marriage and Motherhood: Nurturing and Self-Sacrifice

📖 Titus 2:4-5 – "Then they can urge the younger women to love their husbands and children, to be self-controlled and pure, to be busy at home, to be kind, and to be subject to their husbands, so that no one will malign the word of God."

- Marriage and motherhood bring new responsibilities, joys, and pressures.
- Many women struggle with balancing personal identity, family, and faith.
- Emotional and physical exhaustion can arise from caring for children, managing a home, or navigating career expectations.

◆ **What They Need:** Support, appreciation, shared responsibilities, and spiritual encouragement.

3. Middle Age: Reflection, Transition, and Renewed Purpose

📖 Isaiah 46:4 – "Even to your old age and gray hairs I am He, I am He who will sustain you. I have made you and I will carry you; I will sustain you and I will rescue you."

- Women in this season may feel overlooked or unappreciated.
- They often reflect on past decisions, family growth, and personal achievements.
- Some may experience empty nest syndrome, longing for purpose beyond raising children.

◆ What They Need: Encouragement to pursue passions, emotional reassurance, and acknowledgment of their wisdom and contributions.

4. Senior Years: Legacy, Wisdom, and Spiritual Depth

📖 Proverbs 16:31 – "Gray hair is a crown of splendor; it is attained in the way of righteousness."

- Older women desire companionship, purpose, and reflection on God's faithfulness.
- They often become mentors, grandmothers, and spiritual guides in their families and communities.
- They seek to leave a legacy of faith, love, and wisdom.

◆ **What They Need:** Honor, companionship, and opportunities to share their wisdom with younger generations.

Fictional Example: A Husband Learning to Adjust

A husband noticed that as his wife transitioned into motherhood, she became more emotionally overwhelmed and distant. At first, he felt rejected and frustrated, but then he decided to observe and listen.

He realized that: ✅ She was struggling with physical exhaustion and emotional overload. ✅ She needed reassurance, appreciation, and help with household responsibilities. ✅ When he spoke words of affirmation and offered help, their intimacy and connection deepened.

💡 The lesson? Supporting a woman through her seasons requires patience, understanding, and intentional love.

Key Insights for Husbands

1. Be Adaptable as Life Changes

📖 1 Peter 3:7 – "Husbands, in the same way, be considerate as you live with your wives, and treat them with respect as the weaker partner and as heirs with you of the gracious gift of life, so that nothing will hinder your prayers."

- Seasons change, and so do women's needs—physically, emotionally, and spiritually.
- A wise husband adjusts his support to match his wife's current season.
- Learning to listen, observe, and respond with love strengthens the relationship.

2. Support and Encourage Growth

📖 Proverbs 31:11-12 – "Her husband has full confidence in her and lacks nothing of value. She brings him good, not harm, all the days of her life."

- Encourage her spiritual, emotional, and personal development.
- Celebrate her achievements and God-given talents.
- Offer gentle leadership, not control, to help her flourish.

3. Celebrate Each Season Together

📖 Song of Solomon 2:10 – "My beloved spoke and said to me, 'Arise, my darling, my beautiful one, come with me.'"

- Every stage of life has beauty and purpose.
- Embrace each season as an opportunity to grow closer.

- Celebrate milestones, small victories, and new experiences together.

Final Thoughts

A woman's journey through life is filled with transitions, challenges, and growth. Understanding her seasons allows husbands, family members, and friends to offer the right kind of support, love, and encouragement.

💡 Sisters, each season you walk through is part of God's beautiful design. Embrace it, and allow His grace to guide you.

As you navigate life's seasons, may you find strength, wisdom, and joy in every stage.

Chapter 8:
The Woman as a Life-Giver and Enhancer

Women Nurture and Build

Women were uniquely created to bring life—not only in the physical sense but also emotionally, spiritually, and relationally. A woman's presence in a home, workplace, and community can foster growth, healing, and transformation. Her words, actions, and faith shape the people around her, either uplifting or diminishing their potential.

📖 Titus 2:4-5 – "Then they can urge the younger women to love their husbands and children, to be self-controlled and pure, to be busy at home, to be kind, and to be subject to their husbands, so that no one will malign the word of God."

God calls women to be nurturers and builders, not only within their families but in all aspects of life. Women hold a unique ability to speak life, encourage dreams, and cultivate an atmosphere of peace and faith.

Biblical Example: Mary, Mother of Jesus

Mary, the mother of Jesus, exemplifies the power of a woman's influence. She was not only entrusted to give birth to the Savior of the world but also to nurture and guide Him through childhood and into His purpose. Her faith, wisdom, and obedience played a crucial role in Jesus' journey.

📖 Luke 1:38 – "I am the Lord's servant," Mary answered. "May your word to me be fulfilled." Then the angel left her.

Lessons from Mary:

✓ Women influence future generations through their faith and actions.

✓ God entrusts women with great responsibilities, and their obedience impacts history.

✓ A woman's nurturing presence shapes the calling of those she raises and mentors.

Mary's unwavering faith ensured that she fulfilled her role as a life-giver and spiritual guide for Jesus. Women today have that same calling—to nurture, encourage, and strengthen those around them.

The Power of a Woman's Influence

Women's words and actions set the spiritual and emotional climate of their homes and communities.

1. Women Bring Strength and Comfort

📖 Proverbs 31:25 – "She is clothed with strength and dignity; she can laugh at the days to come."

- Women provide strength in times of adversity and comfort in times of uncertainty.
- A godly woman remains steady, resilient, and prayerful even in challenging situations.
- She understands that her presence and support bring stability to her family.

⬧ **What This Looks Like in Everyday Life:** Encouraging a discouraged spouse, standing strong in faith through trials, and being a source of wisdom and patience for children and loved ones.

2. Encouragement from a Woman Can Transform a Home

📖 Proverbs 18:21 – "The tongue has the power of life and death, and those who love it will eat its fruit."

- Women's words carry incredible power—they can build up or tear down those around them.
- A woman's ability to speak life, inspire confidence, and express gratitude can transform relationships.
- Homes filled with encouragement and kindness flourish with love and security.

⬧ **What This Looks Like in Everyday Life:** A wife speaking words of affirmation to her husband, a mother reassuring her children of their worth, or a friend offering encouragement in difficult times.

3. A Godly Woman Builds, Never Tears Down

📖 Proverbs 14:1 – "A wise woman builds her house, but with her own hands the foolish one tears hers down."

- A wise woman understands that her actions shape the spiritual and emotional foundation of her home.
- She chooses patience over anger, encouragement over criticism, and prayer over complaints.
- God blesses women who seek to build, restore, and nurture rather than criticize or destroy.

◆ **What This Looks Like in Everyday Life:** Speaking to a husband with respect rather than resentment, choosing to resolve conflicts with grace, and creating a peaceful home through **love and faithfulness**.

Fictional Example: A Wife Transforming Her Home

A wife, Sarah, found herself in a difficult season. Her husband was overwhelmed with work, their children were struggling, and their home felt tense.

At first, Sarah responded with frustration. She demanded more from her husband and scolded her children. But then, she felt God calling her to change the atmosphere of her home through prayer, kindness, and encouragement.

She decided to: ✅ Begin each morning with prayer over her home and family. ✅ Speak life-giving words to her husband, reminding him of his strength and leadership. ✅ Create a peaceful and loving atmosphere by focusing on gratitude rather than frustration.

Over time, her home transformed. Her husband became more confident and engaged, her children responded with more respect and joy, and she found greater peace in her heart.

💡 The lesson? A woman's presence shapes the atmosphere of her home. Through prayer, encouragement, and faith, she can transform her household into a place of peace and strength.

Pastor Henry Owens Jr

Practical Ways to Be a Life-Giver and Enhancer

1. Speak Life Over Your Family and Friends

✓ Use words of affirmation and encouragement daily.

✓ Avoid harsh, critical, or belittling speech.

✓ Speak hope, faith, and love over your home.

2. Create a Spiritually Nurturing Environment

✓ Make prayer and worship a regular part of your home.

✓ Model faith, patience, and kindness in front of your children and spouse.

✓ Be a source of strength and wisdom for those who look to you for guidance.

3. Support and Build Up Those Around You

✓ Encourage your husband in his leadership and calling.

✓ Celebrate the achievements and gifts of your children.

✓ Be a mentor or spiritual guide to younger women in your community.

Final Thoughts

Women are called to be life-givers, nurturers, and builders in every area of their lives. A woman who walks in her God-given role brings joy, peace, and transformation wherever she goes.

44

💡 Sisters, your influence is powerful! The words you speak, the faith you carry, and the love you share have the ability to change lives.

As you embrace your role as a life-giver and enhancer, may you continue to bring strength, healing, and encouragement to all those around you.

Chapter 9:
The Importance of Spiritual Leadership

Men Must Lead Spiritually

Spiritual leadership is one of the most vital roles a man must embrace. A man's faith and spiritual strength deeply impact his wife, children, and household. When a man prioritizes God, his family follows, and his home becomes a place of peace, direction, and divine order.

📖 Ephesians 5:23 – "For the husband is the head of the wife, as Christ is the head of the church, his body, of which he is the Savior."

A husband's leadership should mirror Christ's leadership—it is not about control, but about serving, guiding, and loving selflessly. God designed men to lead their families with wisdom and faith, ensuring that their household honors Him.

Biblical Example: Joshua

One of the greatest examples of spiritual leadership in the Bible is Joshua. He was not just a military leader, but a spiritual guide for Israel, ensuring that God remained at the center of the nation's life.

📖 Joshua 24:15 – "As for me and my house, we will serve the Lord."

Lessons from Joshua:

✓ Spiritual leadership starts with personal commitment.

✅ A man must boldly declare and model faith in his home.

✅ A strong leader is one who trusts and obeys God fully.

Joshua understood that a family thrives when it is anchored in God's will. A man who leads his home spiritually protects and strengthens his family against worldly influences.

Fictional Example: A Husband Embracing Spiritual Leadership

John was a hardworking husband and father, but he felt spiritually inadequate. He had always left prayer, church attendance, and Bible study to his wife. However, he began to notice that his family lacked spiritual direction. His children were struggling with their faith, and his wife felt burdened with the responsibility of leading spiritually alone.

One night, John decided to start praying with his family. Though it felt awkward at first, he remained consistent. Over time, he saw his wife's faith strengthened, his children more engaged in church, and his own confidence in God grow. His small step of obedience led to a spiritual revival in his home.

💡 The lesson? A man's spiritual leadership does not have to be perfect—it just has to be intentional.

Principles for Leading Spiritually

1. Pray Over Your Family Daily

📖 1 Thessalonians 5:17 – "Pray without ceasing."

- A strong spiritual leader prays for and with his family regularly.

- Prayer invites God's protection, wisdom, and guidance into the home.
- Men who pray over their wives and children build an unshakable spiritual foundation.

◆ **Practical Steps:** Pray together before meals, before bed, and in times of difficulty. Speak blessings over your children and spouse.

2. Set a Godly Example

📖 1 Timothy 4:12 – "Set an example for the believers in speech, in conduct, in love, in faith, and in purity."

- A man's actions speak louder than his words.
- Children and spouses are watching how he lives out his faith.
- A godly leader is one who walks with integrity, kindness, and discipline.

◆ Practical Steps: Attend church consistently, read the Bible regularly, and lead with honesty and humility.

3. Encourage Your Wife's Spiritual Growth

📖 Ephesians 5:25-26 – "Husbands, love your wives, just as Christ loved the church and gave himself up for her to make her holy."

- A husband should never suppress his wife's faith—he should nurture it.
- Encouraging her spiritually strengthens the marriage and deepens their unity in Christ.

- When a husband supports his wife's spiritual journey, she flourishes.

◆ **Practical Steps:** Pray with your wife, discuss the Bible together, and affirm her spiritual gifts and calling.

The Impact of Spiritual Leadership on the Home

When a man leads spiritually, his home becomes a place of peace, wisdom, and direction. Without spiritual leadership, families often drift into confusion, stress, and worldly distractions.

1. Strengthens the Marriage

✅ Couples who pray together stay together.

✅ Spiritual leadership eliminates unnecessary conflicts and builds trust.

✅ A husband who seeks God's wisdom makes better decisions for his home.

2. Guides Children in Faith

✅ A father's faith greatly impacts his children's spiritual growth.

✅ Kids who see their dad pray and read the Bible are more likely to follow Christ.

✅ A strong spiritual foundation protects children from worldly influences.

3. Brings God's Favor and Blessing

📖 *Psalm 128:1-3* – "Blessed are all who fear the Lord, who walk in obedience to him. You will eat the fruit of your labor; blessings and prosperity will be yours."

✓ God honors men who **lead their families in righteousness**.

✓ Spiritual leadership invites **divine protection, wisdom, and blessings**.

✓ A man who follows God **sets his household up for success**.

Practical Ways to Lead Spiritually

For Husbands:

✓ Take the initiative to pray with your wife.

✓ Read Scripture together and encourage faith-based discussions.

✓ Model love, patience, and spiritual maturity.

For Fathers:

✓ Teach your children the importance of faith.

✓ Pray over them before school, at bedtime, and during challenges.

✓ Lead by example—show them how to live a Christ-centered life.

For Single Men Preparing for Marriage:

✅ Develop a personal relationship with God now.

✅ Learn to serve, protect, and guide others in faith.

✅ Be prepared to lead your future home with wisdom and prayer.

Final Thoughts

Spiritual leadership is not about dominance, but about guidance, protection, and love. A man who leads his home in faith empowers his family to grow closer to God and to one another.

💡 Brothers, your faith matters! Your leadership shapes the future of your family and community.

As you commit to walking in spiritual leadership, may your home be filled with God's presence, wisdom, and unshakable faith.

Chapter 10:
Honoring and Protecting Women

Women Must Be Treated with Honor

One of the greatest responsibilities of men is to honor and protect the women in their lives. Women are not just partners, mothers, and friends—they are daughters of God, created in His image, and deserving of respect, love, and care.

📖 1 Peter 3:7 – "Husbands, likewise, dwell with them with understanding, giving honor to the wife, as to the weaker vessel, and as being heirs together of the grace of life, that your prayers may not be hindered."

This verse does not imply that women are weak but highlights that men have a God-given duty to protect and cherish them. When men honor women, they reflect the heart of God, who values and uplifts His daughters.

Biblical Example: Boaz and Ruth

Boaz stands as a model of godly honor and protection. When Ruth, a widowed foreigner, came to glean in his fields, he could have ignored her. Instead, he provided for her, ensured her safety, and treated her with great respect.

📖 Ruth 2:10-12 – "At this, she bowed down with her face to the ground. She asked him, 'Why have I found such favor in your eyes that you notice me—a foreigner?' Boaz replied, 'I've been told all about what you have done for your mother-in-law since the death of your husband—how you left your father and mother and your homeland and came to live with a people you did not know before.'"

Lessons from Boaz:

✅ Protect the dignity and well-being of women.

✅ Provide security and support without expecting anything in return.

✅ Honor a woman's sacrifices and respect her journey.

Boaz's kindness led to Ruth's redemption and security, and their union became part of God's plan for the lineage of Jesus.

Fictional Example: A Husband Honoring His Wife Through Service

David and Sarah had been married for 10 years. Sarah worked tirelessly to take care of their home and children, but David often took her efforts for granted. One evening, he noticed how exhausted she was and decided to step up instead of expecting her to carry the load alone.

He started helping with household duties, listening more, and expressing appreciation for all she did. Over time, Sarah felt more valued and cherished, strengthening their marriage and deepening their emotional connection.

💡 The lesson? Honoring women is not just about words—it's about action.

Ways to Honor Women Daily

1. Respect and Value Her Voice

📖 Proverbs 31:26 – "She speaks with wisdom, and faithful instruction is on her tongue."

- Listen to her thoughts, feelings, and concerns with genuine interest.
- Encourage her gifts, talents, and ideas instead of dismissing them.
- Make room for her leadership and wisdom in family, church, and community.

◆ Practical Steps: Ask her opinions, affirm her ideas, and show gratitude for her input.

2. Protect Her Emotional and Spiritual Well-being

📖 Ephesians 5:25 – "Husbands, love your wives, just as Christ loved the church and gave himself up for her."

- A man must be emotionally present and supportive.
- Protecting a woman goes beyond physical safety—it includes guarding her heart and mind.
- Encouraging her faith and well-being strengthens her confidence and purpose.

◆ **Practical Steps:** Pray over her, speak words of affirmation, and avoid actions that cause unnecessary emotional pain.

3. Serve Her with Love and Humility

📖 Matthew 20:26-28 – "Whoever wants to become great among you must be your servant… just as the Son of Man did not come to be served, but to serve."

- Love is demonstrated through selfless service.
- A godly man seeks ways to lighten her burdens, not add to them.
- Small, thoughtful acts show deep respect and care.

♦ **Practical Steps:** Help with chores, offer her rest, and show appreciation through small gestures of kindness.

The Impact of Honoring and Protecting Women

When men honor and protect women, society as a whole benefits. Strong, respected women create stronger families, communities, and churches.

1. Strengthens Relationships

✓ Honoring a woman deepens trust and love in marriage.

✓ Encouraging women to pursue their calling enriches families and churches.

✓ Women who feel protected can flourish in their God-given purpose.

2. Teaches Future Generations

✓ Sons learn how to respect and protect women by watching their fathers.

✓ Daughters grow in confidence when they see their worth being honored.

✅ Families that value women create legacies of love and integrity.

3. Reflects Christ's Love

📖 John 13:34 – "A new command I give you: Love one another. As I have loved you, so you must love one another."

✅ Jesus valued, honored, and protected women during His ministry.

✅ A man who follows Christ's example demonstrates true biblical leadership.

✅ Honoring women displays God's love to the world.

Practical Ways to Honor and Protect Women

For Husbands:

✅ Speak kind and affirming words to your wife.

✅ Be faithful, supportive, and emotionally present.

✅ Take responsibility for spiritual and emotional leadership in your home.

For Fathers:

✅ Teach your daughters their worth in God's eyes.

✅ Model respect and protection for women.

✅ Set an example of godly manhood and integrity.

For All Men:

✅ Stand up for women's dignity and safety in all settings.

✓ Support and encourage women's leadership in faith and community.

✓ Be a champion of honor, love, and protection in every relationship.

Final Thoughts

Honoring and protecting women is not optional—it is a biblical mandate. When men rise to the challenge of valuing and uplifting women, they reflect God's love and righteousness.

💡 Brothers, let your actions show the world that godly men honor, respect, and protect the women in their lives.

As you commit to treating women with dignity, may your relationships be filled with God's grace, love, and strength.

Chapter 11:
The Woman as a Reflector

Women Reflect What They Receive

Women are like mirrors, reflecting the love, kindness, or neglect that they receive. A woman's response in marriage, family, and relationships is often shaped by what is poured into her heart. If she is treated with love, respect, and appreciation, she will multiply those qualities in return. If she is met with neglect, harshness, or indifference, it can manifest as emotional withdrawal or pain.

📖 Proverbs 27:19 – "As in water, face reflects face, so the heart of man reflects man."

This scripture reveals a profound truth: a man's actions and words are often reflected back through the heart of a woman. A man who cultivates love, peace, and security in his home will find that same energy reflected in his wife and family.

Biblical Example: Hannah

Hannah, the mother of Samuel, was a woman who reflected the faith and devotion she held in her heart. Despite facing years of barrenness and ridicule, she turned her pain into prayer and worship. She poured out her emotions before God, and her faith was rewarded with a son who became a mighty prophet.

📖 1 Samuel 1:10-11 – "In her deep anguish, Hannah prayed to the Lord, weeping bitterly. And she made a vow, saying, 'Lord Almighty, if you will only look on your servant's misery and remember me, and not forget your servant but give her a son, then I will give him to the Lord for all the days of his life.'"

Lessons from Hannah:

✓ A woman's faith can shape her future.

✓ She reflects the spiritual strength she holds within.

✓ When a woman turns to God, He honors her devotion.

Hannah's story teaches us that a woman's heart reflects the love, faith, or struggles she carries within. A husband, father, or leader who encourages her spiritually and emotionally will see that faith reflected back into the home.

Fictional Example: A Husband's Words and Actions Reflected in His Wife

Michael and Lisa had been married for years, but Michael often took Lisa for granted. He rarely affirmed her, ignored her concerns, and assumed that she knew he loved her without needing to express it. Over time, Lisa became distant, withdrawn, and less joyful.

One day, Michael had a realization: his wife's lack of warmth was a reflection of the way he had treated her. He decided to change the atmosphere in their marriage. He began expressing appreciation, showing affection, and listening attentively. Within months, Lisa began to reflect the love she was receiving.

💡 The lesson? A woman will often mirror the energy, love, and care she receives. If she is nurtured, she will flourish; if she is neglected, she will withdraw.

Insights for Men

1. Pour Love into Your Wife, and She Will Multiply It

📖 Ephesians 5:25 – "Husbands, love your wives, just as Christ loved the church and gave himself up for her."

- When a man loves, cherishes, and honors his wife, she will return that love in abundance.
- Women are natural multipliers—what they receive, they give back in greater measure.
- A woman who is deeply loved will create a home filled with warmth, joy, and peace.

◆ **Practical Steps:** Show affection, express gratitude, and be attentive to her emotional needs.

2. A Secure Woman Creates a Secure Home

📖 Proverbs 31:11 – "Her husband has full confidence in her and lacks nothing of value."

- A woman who feels safe, loved, and valued creates an atmosphere of peace and stability.
- Security is not just financial—it is emotional, spiritual, and relational.
- A man who reassures his wife, listens to her concerns, and supports her dreams will see his home thrive.

◆ **Practical Steps:** Provide emotional reassurance, lead with integrity, and be consistent in your love and support.

3. Your Actions Shape the Woman You Live With

📖 Colossians 3:19 – "Husbands, love your wives and do not be harsh with them."

- The way a man treats his wife shapes her response—harshness breeds distance, but love cultivates closeness.
- Words have lasting power—a single word of affirmation can lift her spirit, while a careless insult can break her confidence.
- A man who values and honors his wife will see her become more loving, joyful, and secure.

◆ **Practical Steps:** Speak with kindness, resolve conflicts gently, and affirm her worth daily.

The Power of Reflection in Marriage and Family

A woman's reflection extends beyond marriage—it affects children, friendships, and entire communities. When a woman is nurtured and supported, she reflects that same strength and love to those around her.

1. In Marriage

✓ A husband's love is reflected in his wife's joy.

✓ A husband's patience is reflected in his wife's peace.

✓ A husband's devotion is reflected in his wife's trust.

2. In Motherhood

✓ A mother's kindness is reflected in her children's behavior.

✓ A mother's faith is reflected in her children's spiritual growth.

✅ A mother's words shape her children's confidence and character.

3. In Community

✅ Women who feel valued create healthier relationships and friendships.

✅ Women who are spiritually strong uplift those around them.

✅ A woman who knows her worth reflects confidence and faith wherever she goes.

Practical Ways to Nurture a Woman's Reflection

For Husbands:

✅ Speak words of affirmation and encouragement daily.

✅ Lead with love, patience, and selflessness.

✅ Create a home where she feels safe, valued, and supported.

For Fathers:

✅ Model respect and honor for your daughter's mother.

✅ Teach your daughters their worth and identity in Christ.

✅ Be present and engaged in their lives.

For All Men:

✅ Treat women with dignity, kindness, and respect.

✅ Support and uplift women in church, work, and community settings.

✅ Be mindful that your words and actions impact how women see themselves.

Final Thoughts

A woman reflects the love, respect, or neglect that she receives. If she is met with kindness and security, she flourishes. If she is dismissed or mistreated, she withdraws.

💡 Brothers, be intentional about the energy you pour into the women in your life. If you sow love, encouragement, and respect, you will reap a home filled with joy, peace, and faith.

As you commit to honoring the women around you, may your relationships be filled with God's grace and goodness.

Chapter 12:
The Ultimate Call – Loving Your Wife as Christ Loved the Church

The Highest Standard of Love

The greatest commandment for husbands is found in Ephesians 5:25:

📖 "Husbands, love your wives, just as Christ loved the church and gave Himself up for her."

This scripture sets the highest standard of love—a sacrificial, unwavering, and unconditional love that reflects the way Christ loves us. Loving as Christ loves is not a suggestion; it is a divine command.

A man who loves his wife in this way will see his marriage flourish, his home filled with peace, and his relationship strengthened through grace and commitment.

Biblical Example: Hosea and Gomer

The story of Hosea and Gomer provides one of the most powerful illustrations of God's redeeming love. Gomer was unfaithful, but God commanded Hosea to continue loving her, reflecting God's relentless love for His people.

📖 Hosea 3:1 – "The Lord said to me, 'Go, show your love to your wife again, though she is loved by another man and is an adulteress. Love her as the Lord loves the Israelites, though they turn to other gods.'"

Lessons from Hosea:

✓ Love is not based on perfection, but on grace.

✓ God calls men to love their wives even when it is difficult.

✓ Forgiveness and commitment are at the core of biblical love.

Hosea's love for Gomer was a mirror of God's unconditional love for us. A husband who embraces this kind of love will transform his marriage into a reflection of Christ's heart.

Fictional Example: A Man Choosing Love Through Hardship

James and Rachel had been married for 15 years, but their relationship had grown cold. Rachel felt unseen, and James felt unappreciated. Arguments became frequent, and emotional distance grew between them.

One day, James read Ephesians 5:25 and realized that he had not been loving his wife as Christ loved the church. He made a commitment to change—not by demanding love in return, but by giving love unconditionally.

He began serving her, listening more, and praying over their marriage. At first, Rachel was skeptical, but over time, she saw the transformation in James. Her heart softened, and their love was restored.

💡 The lesson? A husband's love can redeem and restore, even in the face of difficulty.

Final Lessons on Love in Marriage

1. Love Requires Sacrifice and Commitment

📖 John 15:13 – "Greater love has no one than this: to lay down one's life for one's friends."

- Love in marriage is not about personal gain—it is about giving.
- A man must be willing to sacrifice his time, pride, and comfort for his wife's well-being.
- Just as Christ gave Himself up for us, a husband must give himself fully to his wife.

♦ **Practical Steps:** Put her needs before your own, serve her with joy, and show daily acts of selfless love.

2. Grace and Patience Strengthen Relationships

📖 Colossians 3:13 – "Bear with each other and forgive one another if any of you has a grievance against someone. Forgive as the Lord forgave you."

- No marriage is perfect—grace must be extended daily.
- A loving husband is patient, forgiving, and understanding.
- Christ never stops loving us, and a man should never stop loving his wife.

♦ **Practical Steps:** Choose forgiveness over resentment, practice patience, and approach conflicts with love.

3. Unconditional Love Reflects God's Heart

📖 Romans 5:8 – "But God demonstrates His own love for us in this: While we were still sinners, Christ died for us."

- True love is not dependent on emotions—it is a decision to love unconditionally.
- A godly husband loves his wife even when it is not easy.
- The more a husband loves like Christ, the stronger his marriage will become.

◆ **Practical Steps:** Love without expecting anything in return, pray for your wife daily, and cherish her as God's gift.

Final Thoughts

This book is not just about understanding women—it is about understanding love, leadership, and relationships through God's eyes.

If you want to build a stronger marriage, a healthier family, and a deeper connection with the women in your life, the answer is simple:

🔥 Love as Christ loved.

As you commit to loving selflessly, leading faithfully, and honoring your wife, may your marriage be filled with grace, joy, and the presence of God.

www.ingramcontent.com/pod-product-compliance
Lightning Source LLC
LaVergne TN
LVHW052038080426
835513LV00018B/2374